Animals of the Beach

By Czeena Devera

A crab is at the beach.

A tadpole is at the beach.

A turtle is at the beach.

A seagull is at the beach.

A snail is at the beach.

A starfish is at the beach.

A clam is at the beach.

A lobster is at the beach.

10 A sand dollar is at the beach.

A sandpiper is at the beach.

A penguin is at the beach.

A jellyfish is at the beach.

Word List

crab	snail	sandpiper
beach	starfish	penguin
tadpole	clam	jellyfish
turtle	lobster	
seagull	sand dollar	

A crab is at the beach.

A tadpole is at the beach.

A turtle is at the beach.

A seagull is at the beach.

A snail is at the beach.

A starfish is at the beach.

A clam is at the beach.

A lobster is at the beach.

A sand dollar is at the beach.

A sandpiper is at the beach.

A penguin is at the beach.

A jellyfish is at the beach.

Published in the United States of America by Cherry Lake Publishing
Ann Arbor, Michigan
www.cherrylakepublishing.com

Cherry Blossom Press is an imprint of Cherry Lake Publishing.

Library of Congress Cataloging-in-Publication Data

Names: Devera, Czeena, author.
Title: Animals of the beach / by Czeena Devera.
Description: Ann Arbor : Cherry Lake Publishing, [2019] | Series: Wild things
    | Audience: Pre-school, excluding K.
Identifiers: LCCN 2019006056| ISBN 9781534149823 (paperback) | ISBN
    9781534148390 (pdf) | ISBN 9781534151253 (hosted ebook)
Subjects: LCSH: Seashore animals—Juvenile literature.
Classification: LCC QL122.2 .D478 2019 | DDC 591.769/9—dc23
LC record available at https://lccn.loc.gov/2019006056

Printed in the United States of America
Corporate Graphics

CHERRY BLOSSOM PRESS